Introduction The Bluebell Railway is famed the world over for its historic collections of locomotives and rolling stock, and the pioneering spirit of early volunteers on the line. In 2020, the railway marks 60 years in preservation and, to mark the occasion, this book has been published in that year. Instead of looking at the general history of the railway, it considers instead the locomotive fleet of the railway with images throughout preservation. We'll see visitors to the railway, departed residents and firm favourites as we look through the line's history. The book concludes with a short section on Bluebell locomotives elsewhere. So, sit back and enjoy this pictorial ramble through the Bluebell's fleet.

Front Cover SECR No. 592 heads a vintage train of LBSCR and Metropolitan carriages.

Ashley Smith

Above In this wintery scene, we see No. 1638 and 'Standard Four' tank No. 80151 top and tailing a train of MK1s and one Bulleid carriage.

Ashley Smith

Back Cover Perhaps on the same occasion, No. 80151 is seen in this timeless view.

Ashley Smith

Published by Mainline & Maritime Ltd, 3 Broadleaze, Upper Seagry, near Chippenham, SN15 5EY
Tel: 01275 845012
www.mainlineandmaritime.co.uk   orders@mainlineandmaritime.co.uk
Printed in the UK

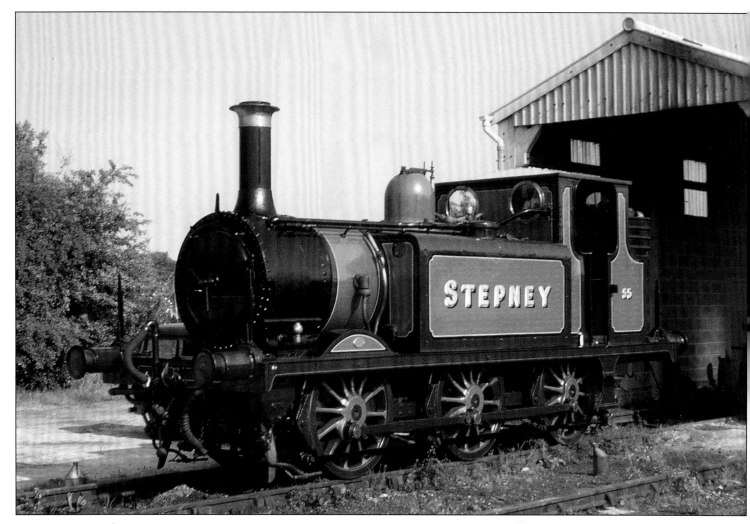

The first standard gauge arrival, and flagship of the Bluebell's fleet is, of course, STEPNEY. This London, Brighton & South Coast locomotive is of the iconic 'Terrier' type and operated the first services on the restored railway in 1960 with P class BLUEBELL. Initially carrying simply-lined black, STEPNEY was soon repainted into the intricate livery of the LBSCR. It is seen here in that livery.

Peter Quilley

Ever since this early period, STEPNEY has been in steam on most of the momentous occasions in the railway's preserved life. In this view, it heads the first train to use Horsted Keynes station; previously trains had stopped short of the station at a specially-constructed halt. At this time, British Railways were still using the station for electric services from Haywards Heath.

Ian Nolan

In this 1963 view, STEPNEY is seen on the rear of a Sheffield Park bound service headed by BIRCH GROVE.

Ron Fisher

The majority of STEPNEY's period in service at the Bluebell has seen it carry the LBSCR livery. This view shows the locomotive in the Horsted Keynes station throat in the guise of the famous Brighton Works 'Terrier', which appeared in golden ochre in the 1950s.

David Ilott

Restored to steam for the railway's 50th anniversary in 2010, STEPNEY only steamed for a short period before being withdrawn for major work. At the close of this 'ticket', the engine was returned to British Railways appearance for photo charter work.

Peter Quilley

The second Southern tank engine type to become synonymous with the Bluebell in this period was the South Eastern & Chatham Railway 'P' class. Only eight were built and four survive into preservation, three on the Bluebell. Appropriately named BLUEBELL, No. 323 'topped and tailed' 1960s trains with STEPNEY until other locomotives were available to compensate for the railway's lack of loop facilities at the northern end of the line.

Ian Nolan

BLUEBELL also lost its drab appearance early on and appeared in this attractive, though not authentic to any of her previous operators, blue. It has subsequently appeared in green and an SECR-inspired lined blue.

Professor Stefan Buczacki

No. 323 saw more extensive use in the 2010s than STEPNEY, heading a variety of Bluebell services either alone or doubleheading. In this view, the engine heads the prestigious Pullman car dining services on the railway. Although diminutive, the locomotive appears appropriate at the head of the splendid train.

Tom Waghorn

No. 27, the second Bluebell 'P' class locomotive, was under restoration at the time of writing with a project ongoing, targeted at ensuring its return to service. The engine is seen here in the mid-1960s when the use of small 0-6-0 side tanks was extensive.

Alastair Wood

It is remarkable that, of the four 'P' class locomotives to survive into preservation, three are located at the Bluebell. The other is a resident at the Kent & East Sussex. No. 178 survived thanks to its sale into private industry, working for the famous Bowaters paper mill in Kent. It returned to Bluebell service in the early 2010s.

Professor Stefan Buczacki

Today, No. 178 carries the full version of the SECR's lined livery.

Paul Bryson

One larger South Eastern & Chatham tank engine, No. 263, survives on the Bluebell. This 0-4-4 is typical of the increasingly large locomotives of the pre-grouping railways for commuter services. It has had several periods in traffic on the Bluebell, is one of several locomotives on the railway that has not operated on another preserved line in several decades and has recently been rendered as a Hornby model.

Professor Stefan Buczacki

Heading a special train for the Canvey Railway Club with No. 592, No. 263 is seen here in simple green livery without the markings or lettering of the SECR. The train includes British Railways suburban coaches still in BR blue which are no longer at the railway.

Ian Docwra

In a more recent scene, No. 263 is seen at Kingscote on a vintage train.

Ian Docwra

The influence of the SECR at the Bluebell is strong and it is the best represented, by far, of any pre-grouping company on the railway. No. 65 has ties to the nearby Kent & East Sussex Railway, where it operated in service and has returned in preservation. It is now painted in the attractive lined-green livery of the SECR. The SECR, made up of two technically-separate companies, was infamously poor, making its choice of locomotive colours questionable against railways like the London & North Western, who were reasonably profitable and whose locomotives were noticeably workmanlike.

John Ellender

The luscious rolling scenery through which the Bluebell operates is shown to beautiful effect in this recent view of No. 65 on a four coach train of vintage stock. The SECR birdcage, a design which fell out of fashion along with the clerestory before the advent of grouping in the early 1920s, is represented in the train.

Kees Wielemaker

In this view, No. 65 and No. 592 (a later and larger 0-6-0 built for the SECR) doublehead. They are rare examples of pre-grouping tender engines to steam regularly in preservation anywhere in the UK, with most others conserved in museums or only serving short operational periods to mark significant anniversaries.

John Ellender

No. 592 is seen here in a gorgeous winter scene shortly after leaving Sharpthorn Tunnel.

Ashley Smith

Although it appears to be another antiquated Victorian tender engine, EARL OF BERKELEY was actually constructed in the mid-1930s for use on the Cambrian Railways network using parts from the Great Western Duke and Bulldog types. The 'Dukedogs' saw service well into the 1950s in North Wales, and No. 9017 returned to the region on a visit to Llangollen in 2009. It has operated at the Bluebell in both GWR green and BR black liveries, and is well travelled having visited the South Devon, Severn Valley and other lines.

Mark Andrews

Seen here departing Horsted Keynes, EARL OF BERKELEY makes light work of a five coach train of Southern stock from a variety of periods.
Kees Wielemaker

'Terriers' have become part of the brand of the Bluebell, with No. 72 FENCHURCH also resident on the line. Many 'Terriers' were sold off as their work on frontline duties began disappearing in the early 1900s, and in this view FENCHURCH carries the lettering of one such operator, the Newhaven Harbour Company.

Alastair Wood

More recently, FENCHURCH's appearance has been backdated with winged smokebox front and Marsh umber livery which superseded the brighter 'improved engine green' of Stroudley. This image shows the locomotive being watered at Sheffield Park.

Charlie Verrall

The Bluebell has found special uses for its smaller locomotives, keeping them in steam where other railways may have sold them on or stopped their restoration. One such use is on spring and autumn observation car trains, as seen here approaching Horsted Keynes with FENCHURCH.

Charlie Verrall

Substantially larger than the 'Terriers' were the E4 tanks of the LBSCR, of which one example is preserved. The Bluebell is home to a number of now-unique machines, including No. 463 BIRCH GROVE, seen here piloting BLUEBELL.

Chris Livings

BIRCH GROVE has worn the Marsh umber livery of the latter-day LBSCR for most of its time in preservation, as seen here in the 1960s in Hosted Keynes.

Ralph Ward

In the mid-2000s, BIRCH GROVE appeared in British Railways lined black, as seen here at Sheffield Park. The livery gives the locomotive a more modern appearance, disguising its Victorian build.

Cliff Jones

During its period in operation in the 2010s, BIRCH GROVE carried the Southern Railway green. It is seen here on the opening day of the East Grinstead extension, donning 'The Blue Belle' headboard present on many noteworthy occasions in the line's history.

Tom Waghorn

BEACHY HEAD is soon to become the Bluebell's first resident new-build. Having struggled with smaller designs of express passenger locomotive and rapidly being left behind by developments on other railways, the London, Brighton & South Coast created a fleet of 'Atlantic' 4-4-2s based on the successful C1 of the Great Northern. The determined group on the Bluebell building one has now worked for 20 years to recreate this iconic type and is close to finishing the job. Donations can be made by searching the internet for the locomotive. This image shows one of the originals, No. 32425 TREVOSE HEAD, in service in the 1950s.

Douglas Lock

The B4 tank engines of the London & South Western, built for a variety of marshalling work, were particularly well known for their duties at the vast port of Southampton. The Bluebell is home to No. 96 NORMANDY, seen here carrying sunshine lettering. For many years, the locomotive carried out the railway's shunting duties at Sheffield Park alone though was out of service at the time of writing. A second class member survives at Bressingham Museum & Gardens in Norfolk.

John Ellender

A number of Victorian and Edwardian locomotive types survived well beyond their natural retirement thanks to the particular nature of certain branch lines and byways. The Adams 'radial' 4-4-2Ts were a prime example of this, with three serving into the British Railways period on the Lyme Regis branch line. The sole survivor, No. 488, is seen here shortly after arrival at the Bluebell and still displaying its BR livery.

Ron Fisher

For a number of years in the early 1960s, the Bluebell hosted visiting railtours using locomotives from its own fleet and guests such as Caledonian Railway No. 123. In this view, No.488 heads such a train along a third-rail electrified line.

Charlie Verrall

The North London Railway is one of a number of smaller pre-grouping companies with only a single surviving locomotive to represent it in preservation, in this case No. 58805 of 1880. It arrived at the Bluebell in the early 1960s.

Nigel Menzies

The Southern Railway's U class moguls were a ubiquitous type seen across the network from Cornwall to London that emerged in the late 1920s. In this view, No.1618 is seen on shed at Sheffield Park. The locomotive's lack of smoke deflectors makes for an interesting comparison with the next image of sister No. 1638.

Peter Brabham

The second U class to survive on the Bluebell is No. 1638, which is seen here.

Cliff Jones

Today, the 4-6-0 types of the Great Western and London, Midland & Scottish Railways are the best remembered, but this wheel arrangement first demonstrated it was the future for steam traction in a noteworthy way on the London & South Western. The 4-6-0 design of this company was perpetuated throughout the life of the Southern and examples remained in service into the 1960s. No. 847, along with several other Bluebell residents, is owned by the Maunsell Society which does an amazing job of preserving the sometimes overlooked history of Southern design before Oliver Bulleid.

Chris Livings

Circular headboards have become a rarity today though they were once commonplace on holiday excursions and business specials. The Bluebell, with its Golden Arrow headboard, has kept the tradition alive and this image shows No. 847 carrying another example at Kingscote.

Paul Bryson

The 'Schools' class of Southern Railway 4-4-0s were far removed from the origins of this wheel arrangement with a modern appearance and performance ability. Three survive in the UK, including this one from the mid-1930s, No. 928 STOWE. It was under overhaul at the time of publication and should be another great Southern design to feature in the railway's operational fleet.

Peter Brabham

Designed by Maunsell, the Q class goods locomotives were utilitarian heavy freight locomotives for which the Southern had a markedly small need for compared to the bulk-carrying companies north of London. It is now in its second period of Bluebell operation during which it has visited other railways such as the Severn Valley.

John Ellender

Showing off the unusual double-faced through platform at Horsted Keynes, this shot shows the arrival of No. 541 in British Railways guise on a demonstration freight.

Ashley Smith

Facing dock traffic at Southampton covered only by ailing B4 tanks like NORMANDY at the end of the Second World War but with limited funds at his disposal, the Southern Railway CME Oliver Bulleid acquired 15 S100 locomotives. These engines had been designed for service on the continent and constructed in America. Southampton was the class stronghold until the mid-1960s, when some were withdrawn and others entered departmental service. No. 30064 has led a quiet life in preservation, and has been out of traffic for several decades at the time of publication.

Professor Stefan Buczacki

Oliver Bulleid's pacifics were quite unlike anything that had come before them when built, demonstrating innovative though often impractical features, and were constructed during the Second World War. The first of the two types was the 'Merchant Navy' class, a heavy mainline loco. The Bluebell was formerly home to No. 35027 PORT LINE, now owned by the Royal Scot Trust based in Crewe.

Les Chatfield

As so many Bulleid Pacifics survive, it is not surprising that many have remained out of traffic for long periods or have never steamed in preservation. The lighter 'West Country' and 'Battle of Britain' types, which were the same design of locomotive but christened with different names, have fared a little better than the larger 'Merchant Navies' which are particularly expensive to restore. The Bluebell is home to a 'West Country' named BLACKMORE VALE which is owned by the Bulleid Society. This shot is of the locomotive carrying the name of Bulleid himself and double-heading with No. 34007 WADEBRIDGE, itself a 'West Country' and owned by a dedicated group.

Kees Wielemaker

Another resident Bulleid at the Bluebell is No. 34059 SIR ARCHIBALD SINCLAIR. Originally constructed with streamline casing like BLACKMORE VALE, No. 34059 was one of many Bulleid pacifics to be remodelled by British Railways, though some did survive in as-built condition until the end of their working lives. The engine draws a festive special in this image. Housing as it does locomotives from a wide spectrum of periods and designers, the Bluebell can legitimately claim to well represent the development of steam traction from the late Victorian era to the end of steam in the 1960s.

Mark Andrews

Had it not have been for the Second World War, it is likely that Oliver Bulleid would have designed a diverse and innovative fleet of steam locomotives for the Southern Railway into the 1950s. In reality, his pacifics were the most famous of his small number of SR designs. Another was the Q1 class of 0-6-0, built with the austerity of the war clearly considered. This locomotive, C1 under the unusual Bullied numbering system, belongs to the National Collection, as does No. 120 and others. Unlike the LSWR T9, however, it did operate on the Bluebell in the 1990s.
Chris Livings

One locomotive which will not steam again at the Bluebell, at least in its original form, is No. 78059. It is being converted into a 'Standard Two' tank, of which none survived into preservation, and thus will give enthusiasts another reason to visit the line. The common nature of parts in the British Railways types, such as boilers, make this a conversion rather than a wholly new build.

Peter Brabham

The 'Standard Four' tender engines came in two variants, the 2-6-0 moguls and the 4-6-0 type, one of which is preserved on the Bluebell. It is seen here in steam at Sheffield Park carrying express headcode.

Alastair Wood

No. 75027 is one of several locomotives now on display in the SteamWorks museum at Sheffield Park, having been cosmetically restored for this purpose in BR lined brunswick green with late crest.

Chris Livings

No. 80151, of the 'Standard Four' tank engine version, has found gainful employment in the service of the Bluebell as so many of its classmates did around the wider Southern region in the 1950s and 1960s. The type has proven so useful in preservation that only a small, and ever-reducing, number of them have not been restored to serviceable condition.

Kees Wielemaker

In a stunning evening train shot, No. 80151 stands in Horsted Keynes on a train of Bullied coaches. A second 'Standard Four', No.80064, has operated at the railway in preservation and was on display at the time of writing.

Tom Waghorn

The Bluebell is home to a third 'Standard Four' tank, No. 80100, which is currently stored awaiting restoration.

Nigel Menzies

Standard Five 4-6-0s were prominent on the former Southern network, and received names here, unlike those which saw service on any other region of BR. CAMELOT is supported by a separate society, though the locomotive's links to the railway are strong. No. 73082 entered BR traffic in 1955, the year of the famed Modernisation Plan, and headed for Barry Scrapyard at the end of its career. The locomotive has the larger style of British Railways tender, used with locomotives on the Southern Region to make up for that area's lack of water troughs.

Paul Bryson

The 9F standard locomotives were in service for a scandalously short period of operation before withdrawal in the 1960s, and No. 92240 was typical of this with a service life of just seven years. It was another Barry Scrapyard survivor, though it has spent relatively little of its time in service at the Bluebell since arriving in the late 1970s.

Peter Brabham

Industrial locomotives have never featured prominently in the operating fleet or collection of engines at the Bluebell Railway. The line was blessed with the 'cream' of withdrawn former mainline locomotives in the early 1960s, acquiring interesting Victorian and Edwardian types like the 'Terriers' and P classes. The Bluebell, though, is home to an important industrial locomotive - SHARPTHORN. Used in the construction of the railway, this Manning Wardle locomotive has not steamed in preservation.

Cliff Jones

CAPTAIN BAXTER is the second industrial resident that remains on the railway today. This Fletcher Jennings 0-4-0 emerged from the works of this small, North West firm in 1877 for a life working in a Surrey limeworks. It is seen here during the early days of preservation at Sheffield Park.

Ron Fisher

CAPTAIN BAXTER was restored to steam in 2010, and has spent time on loan recently to other sites such as the Tanfield Railway and Didcot Railway Centre. Amazingly, for such a small locomotive, it has also worked special Bluebell passenger trains, though more frequently appears on brakevan rides at Horsted Keynes. It made history in 2016 with a visit to the Talyllyn Railway in North Wales. Here, it operated on a short standard gauge section of track installed at the railway's Tywyn Wharf station.

Tom Waghorn

One of the most unusual locomotives to have been based on the Bluebell in the early period of preservation was BLUE CIRCLE. The product of Aveling & Porter, its traction engine ancestry is very clear. From its construction in 1926 the engine spent its working life at a cement works and moved to the Bluebell in the early 1960s. It returned to the railway in 2010 and operated brakevan trips. It has spent periods since at the Battlefield Line and Nene Valley Railway.

Mark Andrews

The use of diesel locomotives was, for several decades, precluded on the Bluebell. Shunting and works trains were managed by steam locomotives, giving engines like NORMANDY a regular role in the line's operations. This changed in the late 2000s, as shunting and trains on the railway's East Grinstead extension were switched to diesel motive power. No. 09018 is seen here at Kingscote.

Nigel Menzies

As diesels began to be more accepted, the railway's use of them and fleet size has grown. For example, the railway now offers diesel galas. Here, No. 09018 appears after a repaint into a more suitable British Railways green livery.

Nicholas Martin

ROCKET, the replica from the National Railway Museum, is seen here on a visit to the Bluebell which it made with a mock-up Liverpool & Manchester Railway third class carriage. It had been built for the Rocket 150 event in 1980.

Charlie Verrall

One of the first visitors to the nascent Bluebell was No. 1247, the Great Northern Railway 0-6-0 saddletank which had been privately preserved shortly before this image. It was of the J52 type, which operated across the GNR network and were particularly famed for their work around Kings Cross. It spent many years travelling to a variety of heritage railways before being donated to the National Collection. Hopes that it may steam again, and thus be able to recreated scenes like this, have been strengthened by the locomotive's inclusion in the operational locomotives strategy of the National Railway Museum, released in 2019.

Ian Nolan

The London & North Eastern Railway's service were principally operated north of the capital, so the visit of an LNER engine to the Bluebell holds little historic precedent. That is not to say that locomotives such as GREEN ARROW, the 2-6-2 express freight locomotive built in the 1930s, are not welcomed. This beautiful image of GREEN ARROW at Sheffield Park in the low sunlight reminds us that however authentic or not the sight of a steam locomotive in this historic station is something to behold.

Nigel Menzies

Perhaps the most prominent visitor to the Bluebell Railway over the last 60 years has been FLYING SCOTSMAN. This record-breaking, 1923-built LNER pacific is known around the globe, and brought its stardom to the Bluebell in 2017, hauling packed eight-coach trains in April that year.

Chris Livings

Above LNER pacifics appeared fairly regularly at Sheffield Park throughout the 2010s, including a visit from Jeremy Hosking's BITTERN. The A4 locomotive's visit marked the conclusion of a boiler certificate at the railway's Giants of Steam weekend in 2015. It has been stored more recently along the coast at Margate, in the former factory of Hornby. After several years of operating small and medium-sized locomotives, the visits of high-profile pacifics has reinforced the railway's leading-light status.

Tom Waghorn

Right UNION OF SOUTH AFRICA, a second Gresley 'streamliner', came to the railway in October 2018. By this time, it was becoming clear that 'number nine' would shortly bow out of service in favour of display in Scotland, and so crowds were sizable.

Andrew Shapland

Although a clear relation of the eastern pacifics which came before it, TORNADO is no ordinary A1 class locomotive. This class was entirely scrapped in the 1960s, and we have one today thanks to the hard work of the A1 Locomotive Trust, who constructed a replica through the 1990s and early 2000s. The engine now tours the country on railtours, and is seen here visiting the Bluebell in 2013.

Tom Waghorn

MAUDE, the North British Railway 0-6-0 goods locomotive, came to the Bluebell on hire in 1999 from Bo'ness and appeared in the remake of the Railway Children. This film also featured No. 473 BIRCH GROVE and No. 592, as well as Jenny Agutter. It is seen here working a short goods train during an event. With so many ubiquitous goods engines of this period similar in appearance, MAUDE fits in well to unusual surroundings.

Andy Louch

B12 No. 8572 has been a more recent visitor, coming to the Bluebell in 2016. The inside-cylindered 4-6-0 is based on the North Norfolk Railway.

Paul Bryson

Compared with his predecessor Gresley, Edward Thompson's period at the helm of the LNER's locomotive policy was short, suffered from the austerity of wartime conditions and he remains a divisive figure with enthusiasts today. His B1 locomotive type, though, was a significant success and two survive today. This one, No. 61306 MAYFLOWER, operates railtours with Steam Dreams and is seen here heading for the Bluebell on a charter.

Ian Docwra

SIR BERKELEY, the Middleton Railway based Manning Wardle, is similar in both style and history to the Bluebell's SHARPTHORN. It was built in 1890 for contracting work and initially preserved at the Keighley and Worth Valley Railway. This 0-6-0 saddle tank now belongs to the Vintage Carriage Trust, who have a museum on the KWVR. It recently featured in the 'Jericho' series, based on the trials and tribulations of the railway navvies who built the Settle & Carlisle.

Cliff Jones

Another rare industrial visitor was Kent & East Sussex Railway NORTHIAM, the Hunslet 'Austerity' type, in 1982. These sturdy tank engines, despite being a favourite of preservationists around the UK for their uncomplicated design and wide availability, have never been regulars on Bluebell services.

Nigel Menzies

The National Trust is not perceived as a natural repository of historic steam locomotives today, but it did amass a small collection in the 1950s and 1960s as important engines were withdrawn from revenue-earning service. One such locomotive was No. 1054, the 1888-built LNWR 'Coal Tank'. Now lovingly cared for by the Bahamas Locomotive Society, the engine visited the Bluebell for an event in 2017.

Andrew Shapland

Charles Fairburn continued the long London Midland & Scottish tradition of building large passenger tank engines with his 2-6-4T design of the postwar period. A number of these tanks were built for the Southern region following nationalisation, making a visit of one appropriate to the Bluebell. Both preserved examples are based on the Lakeside & Haverthwaite Railway in the Lake District and have very rarely left the North West. No. 42085 broke this tendency with time at the Bluebell and Great Central railways in 2010.

Andrew Shapland

George Ivatt, son of the Great Northern engineer Henry, was the last chief mechanical engineer of the LMS, and used his short period in office to produce functional, yet attractive, mixed traffic tanks and moguls. These were perpetuated after nationalisation, with examples found on the Western and Southern regions in the 1950s and 1960s. This one, No. 41312, carries the identity of scrapped classmate No. 41282 / 41284 on a visit to the Bluebell in 2006 from its home, the Mid Hants Railway.

Mark Andrews

William Stanier's 8F locomotives replaced a complex range of outdated pre-grouping types on the London, Midland & Scottish network in the 1930s and 1940s. They were the design of choice for military railways in the early Second World War, a large number going abroad, and many were built for use on the overstretched systems of other companies such as the LNER. No. 48624 was an appropriate Bluebell visitor in 2016, having been built nearby in Ashford by the Southern.

Paul Bryson

A famed Great Western 4-4-0, and unofficial holder of the prestigious '100mph-breaking steam locomotive' title, came to the Bluebell in late 2006. No. 3440 CITY OF TRURO emerged from Swindon in 1903, quickly becoming a star performer on the fiercely competitive Ocean Mail trains between Plymouth and the capital. It is now part of the National Collection, and has spent several periods in steam through preservation. This evening shot shows it paired with the Bluebell's resident GW 4-4-0, the nominally-younger EARL OF BERKELEY, at Sheffield Park.

Mark Andrews

On loan from the South Devon Railway, we see No. 3205, a Collett 'goods' type of the 1930s. This popular locomotive is out of service awaiting overhaul at the time of writing, having spent time at the Battlefield Line, Severn Valley and Llangollen, as well as the Bluebell, during its last boiler ticket.

Nicholas Martin

The pannier tank concept became synonymous with the Great Western Railway, and was adapted through a range of iterations. The 57XXs were the most recognisable, having a variety of claims to fame, including a number seeing out their working lives with London Transport. 1939-built No. 3650 came to the Bluebell in 2012, on loan from the Great Western Society at Didcot.

Ashley Smith

Built to operate on the extensive system of South Wales colliery-serving railways of the Great Western after grouping in 1923, the 56XX tank engines are powerful 0-6-2 side tanks. This example, No. 5643, visited the Bluebell Railway for the 2014 season, courtesy of its owners, the Furness Railway Trust.

Ashley Smith

A third GWR tank engine to visit the Bluebell recently is No. 5521, though in a rather unusual livery! Celebrations for the 150th anniversary of the Metropolitan Railway's opening had called for the repainting of this 45XX into the maroon of the MR, and it is seen here on a subsequent visit to the Bluebell in 2013. The engine had, not long before, spent a period in operation on the steam-hauled commuter trains of Wolsztyn, Poland.

Ashley Smith

GLADSTONE, the elegant 0-4-2 express engine of the London, Brighton & South Coast Railway, is seen here on display at the Bluebell in the 1980s. These engines were conceived as a response to growing express traffic. The locomotive was the first to be saved by a private organisation, the Stephenson Locomotive Society, in the 1920s and is now part of the National Collection.

Nigel Menzies

The London and South Western Railway, having avoided the hard fighting for traffic in the South East of England, has not permeated the collection of the Bluebell as much as the LBSCR or SECR. As we have seen, the railway does have a small number of LSWR representatives, and was once home to No. 120, the ex-LSWR T9 of 1899. These impressive locomotives were known for their turn of speed and rebuilding with superheaters, although changing their appearance, did mean the engines survived into service with British Railways. Having been displayed on the Bluebell Railway for some years in the 1990s and early 2000s, the engine went on to the Bodmin & Wenford in Cornwall, where the class was prominent in the 1950s, and then the Swanage Railway. It is seen here, though, during an early visit having brought a railtour to the line in the early 1960s.

Ian Nolan

The Beattie well tanks were also brisk machines, dating from the 1870s. Heavily rebuilt, three remained in service into the 1960s on the Wenfordbridge branch and two were subsequently preserved. This example, No. 30587, visited the Bluebell in 2019 and is seen here with LSWR 0-4-4T CALBOURNE.

Barry Austin

CALBOURNE, another LSWR visitor, had a more complex journey than most to reach Sheffield Park, including a journey on a ferry! The Isle of Wight Steam Railway calls this locomotive, of the O2 class which were so linked with the lines of that island, a resident and loaned the locomotive to the Bluebell in 2019 for an LSWR-themed branch line weekend.

Barry Austin

No. 925 CHELTENHAM, owned by the National Railway Museum, is a member of the 'Schools' type like Bluebell resident No. 928 STOWE and is seen here during a gala visit from its home, the Mid Hants Railway.

Nicholas Martin

EDDYSTONE, the rebuilt West Country pacific, spent late 2006 and 2007 on loan to the Bluebell. This evocative image shows the locomotive leaving on a Kingscote-bound service, nothing of note here denoting that this shot was not actually taken in the Indian summer of Southern steam. The fading light accentuates the vivid colour on the train's Pullman cars.

David Ilott

Here, we see a second image of EDDYSTONE on a similar train. You can almost hear the distinctive Bulleid chuff! The train is notably topped and tailed in the manner of early Bluebell operations.

Cliff Jones

Although the Bluebell remains perhaps the 'purest' railway for steam fans, with no timetabled diesel services in its calendar as of 2020, it has taken the opportunity brought by the presence of diesels on the line to diversify revenue. One result has been the introduction of popular diesel galas. Considered by many to be the ultimate in diesel traction, the 'Deltics' were a small class of just 22 locomotives but they were responsible for top link East Coast expresses through the 1960s and early 1970s. Six survive today, excluding the prototype. No. 55019 ROYAL HIGHLAND FUSILIER is seen here during a 2015 gala, at which it was joined by D9009 ALYCIDON. They have subsequently returned to the line.

Ashley Smith

Another diesel gala scene here with class 50 locomotive No. 50049 DEFIANCE at Horsted Keynes in striking British Rail blue with large logo. Trackwork is being carried out on the adjacent platform road as DEFIANCE stands by. The railway did not remain long enough in British Railways ownership to see locomotives in this livery in service on it.

Nigel Menzies

In this image, we see the West Coast Railways stalwart No. 47580 on a railtour. This locomotive has visited the railway at least twice on such duties, along with a host of others on similar workings.

Andrew Shapland

TYPHOON, perhaps imaginable as the name of a huge express or heavy freight locomotive, is actually a 15 inch gauge pacific from the Romney, Hythe and Dymchurch Railway. It visited for the 50th annivesary in 2010 and Flying Scotsman events in 2017 and is seen here on display.

Mark Andrews

Bluebell locomotives have travelled to a number of other railways in preservation, particularly in recent years. One example is the forays by No. 323 BLUEBELL to the Spa Valley, Severn Valley and elsewhere. It is seen here on an extended visit to the Battlefield Line in Leicestershire.

Peter Coleman

No. 178, the second of the Bluebell's working 'P' class locomotives in the 2010s, spent a lengthy period at the National Railway Museum in York towards the end of the decade. It is seen here on an earlier visit to the Tanfield Railway in 2014.

Alan Burkwood

Covering for a shortage of suitable steam motive power, CAPTAIN BAXTER ventured into the home counties in 2018 with this visit to the Didcot Railway Centre. It shared the shed with a great variety of GWR machines and repaid the courtesy extended by the Great Western Society with No.3650's earlier Bluebell adventure.

Alan Burkwood

On a foray into the West Country, No.73082 CAMELOT is seen at Minehead on the West Somerset Railway with a resident DMU in 2018.

Geoff Perrin

In 2012, a large celebration of railways was held over two weeks at the National Railway Museum. 'Railfest' saw dozens of locomotives sent from around the UK with STEPNEY representing the Bluebell.

Christopher Teague

Visiting for a popular gala event in early 2017, here we see No. 541 in British Railways livery at the Great Central Railway, Loughborough.

Alan Burkwood

Seen on a photo charter at the South Devon Railway during a visit in 2011, No.9017 heads a recreation milk train.

Peter Quilley

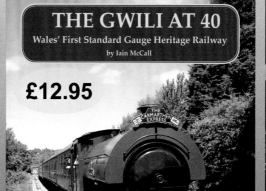